The
Puppeteer's Daughter

Ann Perrin

best wishes
from
Ann Perrin
x

ISBN 978-1-326-68319-1

Dearest Alice in Wonderland

I first met you when I was very young. I learned of all your amazing encounters when my mother read to me from her precious 1926 edition of your book she had won as a prize for 'good conduct' at the local state primary school. You, the white rabbit and people like the maddest of hatters accompanied me on my life's journey. My father was one, as were various uncles and, in my 30s, there was a lecturer at teacher's training college. He even wore a yellow cravat and green check trousers. He was one of the people who persuaded me that life is strange and like the Cheshire cat some things can appear and disappear without warning.

Love from Ann

CONTENTS

Miss Lottie's Last Chance

The Puppeteer's Daughter

Postman's Park

The Yellow House

Miss Lottie's Last Chance

In the kitchen

Let's draw daffodils
and talk about compassion,
capture papery parcels
that hold the tightly packed
buds still green in their pods.

Let our pencils trace
the shapes of ambitious petals
intent on jumping the gun,
reaching out to the world
before their traditional season.

Let's fill in the details
on their frilly faces
add a few shadows,
for they had no say in the matter
like us simply here in this kitchen
at this particular time.

Miss Lottie's Last Chance

She sets the brim of her straw hat
at what she hopes is a rakish angle,
brushes bits of twig from her brown
cotton skirt, pulls the arms of her holey
cardie closer like a hopeful hug.

She climbs on a stool and places
bits of stray string into a rusty tin,
wipes secateurs with an oily rag,
seals half-opened seed packets, placing
them into an obliging array of jars.

She takes a swig of a brandy from a bottle
marked for emergencies, while a grumpy owl
painted on a shopping bag glares.
She makes short shrift of him shaking the bag
upside down to dislodge lurking spiders.

From the corner of her eye she catches
sight of her old black wellies, blushes
at the memory of sitting, only yesterday
on her bench, near to tears, her limbs
too soggy with fatigue to pull them off.

How lucky that an old gent on his bike
was passing and joined in the tussle.
Today she slips out of her old gardening shoes,
watches a flock of rogue cockatiels
spreading their wings and taking flight.

Lizzie

swept the floor
all morning
for something to do.
Janey Jones
fed the baby goat,
her folk out calling.

Paul, a tall dark kid
rode horses bareback.
Jakey tried to train
a hawk, Danny whittled
wood and Frankie
sang sad songs.

Old man Smith banged
the trailer door
with his stick. "Ann"
he called "get those kids
a learning."

When they burned
her caravan, she only took
granny's sewing scissors.

The Lace Maker

I found the brown hessian lace cushion
in the loft wrapped in crumpled tissue paper
the pattern and pins still in place
wooden bobbins, one with buttons
on the metal ring instead of
the more traditional spangles
a tiny flat mother-of-pearl button
from a nightgown, another cut
from a man's shirt, a round brass metal
moulded button from a soldier's
uniform.

Fine white cotton led to the last
twist in the pattern that her wrinkled
brown hands would ever make.

Unholy

I want to go to Prestatyn
where my mother proudly pushed the black Marmet pram
my grandmother had sent by train from London

I want to go to Prestatyn
where a landlady shunned a single mother
cradling a frail body in her arms

I want to go to Prestatyn
to see the house if it's still standing
where a Mrs Shuttlebottom agreed to take my mother in

I want to go to Prestatyn
to find the church where my mother borrowed the bible
the dusty one I discovered the other day

stamped inside the cover
not to be taken away.

Secrets

this clock is left in memory of my son
lost at sea to you his first and only love

a dream woke her from a lifetime's sleep
like Cinderella she missed its chime
but the fairy godmother watched and waited

years passed cogs and wheels
fell out of alignment, the keys vanished
but the people on its watery landscapes
kept walking the roman numerals lost their shine

inside the dark hollow case
heavy weights faltered fell to the carpet
hidden by brown polished doors
finely balanced on broken hinges

now for the last time she paused
lifted the door, peered inside
like a nun finding an abandoned orphan
saw this note pasted inside

this clock is left in memory of my son
lost at sea to you his first and only love

Afraid of the dark

From my bedroom under the eaves,
in total darkness I creep down
the tiny wooden staircase, clinging
to the banisters to reach the landing
below, feel the flecked wallpaper
bubble beneath my fingers, cord carpet
teases my toes, reach the bathroom,
turn the handle, hear the door creak
a weary welcome, trace my way
along the cold copper pipes,
until I see the flicker of light
from the ancient ascot water heater
as it groans alone in the green
tiled bathroom. I move forward
to the lavatory door, into the dark
damp room. I hear the wind whistle,
the howl of ghosts
that linger on the coal shed
in the blackened night.
I take the last desperate steps.
Just in time,
I let the icy pan numb my bum
as warm pee makes
a comforting ring
falling into the waiting pool.
Tearing one sheet of wickedly
sharp toilet paper,
my hand swings out
to the wooden handle
of the heavy chain,
pulling it down so hard
that if it were Sunday church bells
would surely chime.

Needles

The house is full of needles
from my mother
rows and rows of them
in different sizes
Millards, Sharps, Dorcas,
some sticking optimistically
awaiting their next task
needles for darning socks
needles for threading beads
wide-eyed needles for daisy
chain or stem stitch embroidery
so here I am on my hands
and knees, steel wand at the ready
mending a magic carpet.

A Fairy on the 12A

There was a fairy on the 12A today
with white gauzy wings,
purple tights and pink wellingtons.
Her magic powers spread
to the lady with the new hip giving her gyp,
because she smiled.
Two old women who staggered on the bus,
with heavy bags exchanged cheerful glances.
An old man in a flat cap who had long ago
given up believing in fairies started humming.
A middle-aged woman with pearl earrings
stopped tapping her mobile.
A young woman looking out of the window
lost in her own thoughts turned round,
she could see her whispering spells
into her baby brother's ear,
hear his excited gurgles
spilling over the sides of the buggy,
floating like bubbles along the aisle.

Great Aunts

Aunt Ive typed her life story
on an old Remington with two
fingers so it took a very long time.

I inherited Aunt Ethel's biscuit
cutters in a metal box each one
fitting neatly inside the other.

When Aunt Con died, her sister
talked to her chair as though
she was still there.

She wasn't mad just lonely
both sisters had lost their
sweethearts in the Great War.

One day a charity race balloon
landed in the garden with a tag.
She contacted the address.

A boy of ten called Charlie
called to collect it and she made
a friend for the rest of her life.

Ambition

I've not flown to New York
but I've taught gypsies to read
and watched Rosie bottle-feed
a newborn goat.

I've not gone on a cruise,
been seated at the captain's table
but I've crossed the Channel in a tiny
yacht with some two-bit actors
who promised they could sail.

I've not run barefoot over hot coals
but I've wandered the Argonne Forest
dodging unspent ammunition
giving thanks for simply being alive.

The Sunday School Outing

The first time many London children had seen the sea.
Those given tiny pictures of Jesus with a prayer for
good attendance climbed into the charabanc with
a packed lunch wrapped in pieces of washed cotton.

Girls clung to friends boys scrambled to the back
singing 'Oh we do like to be beside the seaside' to pass
the time until Miss Blossom insisted on something more
suitable like 'Jesus bids us shine with a clear bright light'.

On arrival we'd huddle on ex-army ground sheets braver
girls tucked Sunday best dresses into school knickers to
paddle while boastful boys discarded shoes and socks to run
headlong into the waves wet through for the rest of the day.

At one o'clock precisely it was time to eat Marmite sandwiches
to sip weak orange drinks before dedicated helpers snatched
a nap and we'd creep away to annoy crabs and build sand
castles towers and turrets to decorate with slipper shells.

Pocket money collected in advance and added to church
funds ensured every child queued for ice cream
buoyed with confidence it was time to bury the lay preacher
up to his shoulders in the sand.

Swings and Roundabouts

trailing over Hampstead Heath
to the fair, the music drifting up from
the roundabouts, the thrill of the swing
boats, rifles at the ready for men to be
men and knock down the moving targets
in an attempt to win a solitary goldfish
in a plastic bag, the hoopla with furry
toys impossible to win, the mechanical
bird sitting in his gilded cage singing his
clockwork song ready to pick a fortune
written on a tiny piece of paper for a
threepenny piece placed in a gypsy's
hand

For love of Jonathan 1955

outside the Old Vic
intent on getting a seat in the gallery
we exchange sidelong glances
a busker's fingers dance on the yellowed
keys of the accordion
my companion's baggy linen jacket
shouts intellectual the threadbare knees
of his cords whisper beware
later full of language and laughter
we idle across Westminster Bridge
watch the reflections of the city
melt into the depths of the Thames.

Water is Amazing

Sea fret in Scarborough
    like a veil
  of sorrow in memory
     of Ann Bronte
drifting
      in a pedalo
  in Crystal Palace Park
      bare feet
    warming in the sun
catching
   a mackerel
      seeing such sad
reproachful eyes
     for the first time
the old man hiring
    model yachts
    in the Tuileries
   to set sail on Sundays
a wild tide
     that snatched
      the tiny village
leaving a beach
    of mother of pearl
waves falling from the frame
      drowning the woman
  in the green
     satin dress
climbing
    the boards
  of the blackened wreck
   where a child
     without speech
    finds her voice.

In the Balance

May, they say, is full of promise.
We have just two straggly bluebells and how long
before a late frost saps newly planted fragile shoots
and will the robin's eggs in the nest survive, balanced
precariously between tins of fertiliser and Weedol
on a shelf in the greenhouse?
A sleek ginger tom eyes the birds eagerly
from under the hedge whilst I, like a demented
guardian angel, attempt to fix an accessible
temporary door with sticks and chicken wire.
Now the growbags will not get planted and dreams
of the heady fragrance of ripening tomatoes
all summer long, drift into the mist of secret longings.
The robins' beaks now full of curious green insects,
cautious at first, fly through gaps in the wire.
The cat stiffens, glares, his mouth tightens, he crawls
reluctantly back under the hedge.

Green Fingers

I light the candle
on my mother's allotment
on the day of her funeral
and watch the tiny flame glow
let her spirit wander
to where we'd pick
the first raspberries
I bend the boughs of the damson tree
to pluck the fat black fruit
see her gaze hopefully
at strawberry runners
pile manure on to roots of rhubarb
she is here
ready to fall into
the soft brown earth.

The Puppeteer's Daughter

Ancestry

My people were
in the rag trade
their trademark
a thimble.
Granddad had
a fruit shop
his trademark
a black cash box
and constant cough.
An ancient uncle
mixed pigments
for Windsor and Newton
and studied the great masters.
Gran's folk came
from gypsy stock
fortune tellers
and dreamers.
Dad had a dance band
during the war
and played for radio Milan.
My mother lived
by her needle
and cooked
the lightest ever
Victoria sponge.

The Puppeteer's Daughter

The Mad Hatter's eyes
in rubber sockets,
no longer rolling, and minus
his mad mutinous expression
greet mine. His stout top hat,
crimson jacket, silk cravat
and tough rubber boots
challenge my decision.
Come on he pleads.
I'm old and homeless:
Am I really to be abandoned
to a Yellow box storage unit?

'Give them bread and circuses'
but now I bury the circus in boxes.
Charlie the clown
with his bumptious greeting,
Nicky with gentle manner
always one step behind the logic,
his butterfly net never actually
trapping the colourful wings.
Popov based on a real Russian
clown, walked a tightrope,
his antics created a common
language.

No sense left in the caterpillar now
his scales have disintegrated.
How I choked when for the last
time, I took an unfamiliar drag
breathed smoke down the tiny tube
"So who are you?" he groaned.
He may well ask.

Carving

Lime hands
mine enfold
my father's
both have
first fingers
missing
splintered
lost in the
50 years
that set
us apart.

All Sorts

Everyone helped on Christmas Eve, the children in the living room
trusted to make neat crosses on sprouts bottoms,
peel potatoes and prod the hot chestnuts

We'd laugh at my mother's story of corn beef roast during the war.
Now a few years on it was a roast chicken killed by Grandma
out in the garden and hung in the scullery for two days

Grandpa staggered up the hill from the underground at eight
with apples, pears and nuts from our greengrocers in Goodge Street,
gifts from fellow shopkeepers, glace fruits our absolute favourite

Grandmother insisted all through the war there would be no black market;
her Methodist beliefs could not sanction anything dishonourable.
"Pity," said Uncle Jack in later years, "We could have had butter, eggs,
all sorts."

Wonderland

Sprawled on the kitchen table
the Mad Hatter
his top hat
covered in papier-mâché
a newsprint
picture of Putin,
the March Hare
missing an ear,
Alice in Victorian
lace knickers
awaits her dress
washed and drying
on garden wire
hanging over the sink.
The White Rabbit,
checking his pocket watch
in the perfect condition
he was 30 years ago,
has plenty of time.

The North Pier Blackpool

'It's a small world' for our marionettes,
three shows daily on the North Pier.

Our parents busy, we take stock - the mighty
black tower, the circus and ballroom.

Donkeys stand in line ready for a ride
trams trundle along the promenade.

Crowds gather on the famous golden mile, kiss me
quick hats, tuppence to see a mermaid.

The man from Mars in a bright green jump suit
is surreptitiously eating a big cream bun.

And so the season goes on, families from the mills
the mines and the factories, everyone laughing.

Clapping from the back

sent out to watch the show
so as not to get in the way
wooden butterflies danced
to the Nutcracker Suite
suddenly they became bright
and luminous red and orange
wings shimmered as dad
switched on his newly
acquired fluorescent lights
jumping up clapping with
excitement I suddenly heard
the whole audience was joining in.

Music From Another Room - 1948

Flying through banks of clouds, sucking barley sugar
off to Paris to stay with Madame Roy and daughter Juliette
father's war time friends. Bonjour, bonjour
polite exchanges, cups of English tea.

Madame throws open her kitchen window to reveal
on a white cloth, my mother's home made cake
carried from London. Neighbours gather, "ooh la la"
"c'est magnifique," plant wet kisses on our cheeks.

Music seeps in from another room, my father
not used to playing second fiddle to anyone
let alone my mother and her cake is playing La Mer
on Madame's baby grand, we move to the sitting room.

Family portraits hang on the wall, father's performance
is applauded, pieces of cake passed round, while Juliette
stands close to father and sings in perfect English
'Pedute Cose' a love song he wrote during the war.

In the days that follow we visit the Eiffel Tower
jog along the streets in a horse drawn cab, wander
Montmartre, watch artists fill canvasses with bold colours
bow our heads as we enter the Sacre Coeur.

We learn how to row on the lake near Versailles
every detail captured on father's 8mm movie camera
but the highlight, the Théâtre de Paris, where a tiny figure
dressed in black takes stage, picks up the microphone,

'L'Accordeonniste' 'Je ne regrette rien.'
for this is the little sparrow of **Paris** Edith Piaf
the audience stand, they shout 'Bravo, Bravo,'
she bows her head, smiles, reaches out in a final gesture.

The grown ups chatter, father in perfect French
they gather their things, my mother is ahead I follow
glancing back I see my father reach out and clasp
briefly Juliette's hand.

Years later when I recall Paris, the apartment, my father's
passion for the music of the age, Juliette looking down at him
as he played, I realise for a brief moment he may have had
all he ever wanted.

Minding Grandpa

Grandpa sits in silence twisting threads on a white
wooden frame with rows of neat nails on each side

weaving patterns with silky thread recovering
from the Great War and comrades lost on the Somme

forbidden by Grandma from talking
of gas, madness or months of recuperation.

Memories fall into the safety of the sitting room
shiny bodkins glint in the sun like bayonets

his fingers unroll a length of gold as tales of the dead
suddenly return and his eyes fill with tears.

He whispers to me about a hospital ship blown to pieces
and jabs a line of blue twine into the emerging mat.

A screech from his green parrot breaks his sombre mood.
He smiles and ties a golden knot in triumph.

Polly pads along his arm, sings 'Roll out the barrel.'
I gather up Grandpa's wayward threads.

Weaving Spells

He was a magician to us
weaving spells with wood and clay.
Other people's dads went to work
and reappeared for supper

Ours spent his days
and most nights
carving marionettes
in this cluttered workshop.

He was always engrossed
kneading clay or carving wood.
the music of Glenn Miller blaring
from a battered radio.

We would clink through the chaos
with mother's homemade cakes,
the smell mingling with the stench of glue
boiling on an ancient cooker.

Our faces shone with shy smiles
as his hand took the teacup.
He had been whisked away to war,
we barely knew him.

We lived at Gran's
and discovered him one day
in the hallway
with a battered trunk.

A soldier
a coarse khaki uniform
a clarinet in a case
and chocolate in his pocket.

First published in 'Don't Throw away the Daisies'

Annie

Grandma's treadle sewing machine marked out her status
and her territory. Her body fitted perfectly, the rhythm of her feet
on the plate clanking as it coaxed the whole thing into action.
She loved buying materials in the January sales, savouring
the moment, placing the paper pattern on the cloth, pinning,
cutting, tacking, threading until the intricate garment emerged.
I can see her now in the hallway hurriedly putting the final touches
to our holiday dresses as Dad was revving our old Standard
ready for the journey.

She bred blue budgerigars in a spare room, seven cages
of screeching pairs with dark eyes and sharp beaks.
She checked the nesting boxes each day, replacing the sand trays,
filling pots with clean water, full of smiles when a scrawny
baby bird with hooded eyes had pecked its way into a fragile world.

The Flower Seller

The old flower seller
at Waterloo
threw a posy of violets
and primroses into
the Prince of Wales'
horse drawn carriage
got arrested
but then a pardon
from the Queen.
She tied it to her
flower basket
for the rest
of her life.

Teaching gypsies
Tracy once told me
her granny was
a flower seller
at Waterloo
one day she said
she never came home.

Lifelines

1

Mrs Lever lived in Balmour Street
she whitened our front step
and polished the door knob
once a week on Saturdays.
It wasn't that we had servants
just Grandpa had a fruit shop
in London and Mrs Lever
had been left a widow
with seven children.
Grandpa said Mrs Lever
would turn her nose up at charity
letting her earn a few bob was
the least we could do.

2

Aunt Daisy married above her station
and went to live in Dorset. She had
her own dressmaking business.
When we were evacuated to Sandbanks
we never saw the sea but wandered
all over her house with huge oil
paintings on the wall and a garden
with pools and a stone statue of a child
with arms outstretched.

3

There was a life-sized
stuffed brown bear
standing in the entrance
to Marshall and Snellgrove
with sad glass eyes
and a chain across
to protect the public.

Wakes Weeks
(The annual holiday for mill workers)

Over the season   fifteen thousand mill   workers and miners
listened to the aria   from Madam Butterfly mimed to a record
by a marionette   in a pale blue   silk kimono.

Laughing in the line

Too soon the school bell rings summoning me to a stark
red brick building where tight featured war widows teach.

Mrs Thomas hovers like a thin angular spider, knitting
her lost love into a continuous web of plain and pearl.

Milk congeals on the radiator, a sour sickening smell,
as I copy the white chalked words into my exercise book.

In my own world I do not hear the playtime bell,
the rule of silence. Breathless I stand laughing in the line.

The blows from the slapping sting and the sense of injustice
lasts a lifetime.

Green

The stand up at the Komedia says
        'What is green and bounces up and down?'
That first season in show business in Eastbourne when she dyed
her hair blonde her aunt locked her out of her flat thinking she
was no better than she should be
        her mother rushed down to see what was going
on insisted she died her hair back to brown and it turned a ghastly
shade of green but one of the guys that played the tubular bells
with his brothers really fancied her and her hair and she lost her
senses in a beach shelter.

The stand up at the Komedia says
        'What is green and bounces up and down?'
Trailing the agents in the Charing Cross Road in the 50s with a
basket of marionettes, a violinist and an egg laying ostrich, three
Can Can girls but enough savvy to sidestep the casting couch
        Mr A was rumoured to look after chorus girls in
caravans promising them a chance to appear in the movies but
really a tour of working mens clubs or a brief appearance at
Chatham Empire or Leeds City of Varieties she told him she had
dancing parrots that sung and he said 'I'll let you know.'

The stand up at the Komedia says
        'What is green and bounces up and down?'
Auditioning at The Windmill dodging bare breasts and giant fans
Sheila van Damm not even promising 'to let you know' thus rejecting
        the velvet stripping cat, the spider flirting with a
fly to the sound of Peggy Lee singing 'Fever.' Mr T with an
upmarket Cabaret Club behind Simpsons of Piccadilly loved the
violinist, the ostrich, the Can Can girls, the cat, spider and the fly.
But Mr C enticed the dancers away for a chance to appear in
Espresso Bongo.

London to Crewe

Age can play tricks so can it be true
did I travel from London to Crewe
with baskets of puppets marked 'handle with care'
a tip for the porter, a second-class fare?

Did the windows flop open for final goodbyes
for a mother to weep and a lover to sigh?
I know people waved as the train pulled away
and we settled in seats in an orderly way.

I can see the old men with a neat deck of cards
as we trundle past houses, factories, yards.
I remember the carriage where the rich could eat
while a man shovelled coal in the dirt and the heat.

A village, a river, a church with a spire
as smoke and smut rose from the blaze of the fire.
I believe that we reached every station on time
the guard guarding luggage and those baskets of mine.

Sometimes I'd run through each part of my show
think of some changes and how they might go.
I'd check the address for my digs for the week
and might even drift off for a few moments sleep.

But plenty of laughter when I change at Crewe
and stars such as Eric and Ernie pass through.

Letterpress

The old Adana
never stopped clanging
virgin paper fed its jaws.
Nearby large drawers held
sets of single letters in
Garamond or **Dorchester**
for straight talking
Venetian Gothic, curvy
and romantic
for invitations.

Typesetting done
sheets destined to be
hand-fed between rubber rollers
emerge in sticky black ink
publicity flyers, leaflets
programmes, plays for
Pelham Puppets
all laid out on every
available space to dry.
We did everything ourselves
to cut costs.

A hundred years ago
TJ Cobden-Sanderson threw
all the type from Dove Press
into the Thames when he fell out
with his partner.

137 Bus

We are travelling
on the top
of the 137 from
the Archway
to the West End
to collect a new
type face from
the Adana shop
so why on the
way home are we
hugging
a deep blue
ceramic dish
full of tiny pebbles
a soapstone hill
two small houses
a mirror pond
a bridge and
tiny Japanese lady
with a red parasol.

Shadows

it feels heavy in her hand
the opaque glass ball
twice the size of a marble
she peers at the many reflections
cast by spirals of light and movement
from the busy street outside the window
her head an upside down shadow

twirled in her fingers pink and mauve
a shimmering yellow a hazy green
now she sees a long thin line running across
the centre reminding her of the West Pier
as it was in the sixties yes the sixties
with the sunset falling into the sea

she recalls they ordered oysters
at the Regency watched starlings
settle on the roof of the domed ballroom
squeezed lemon slices shattered the claws
of the red crab unaware that this would mark
the end of an era

her fingers spin over the surface of the ball
her thumbnail finding a fine indentation
she traces the line seeking answers
but the protagonists are long gone
their understudies too moved on
the opaque glass ball keeps its secrets
her head an upside down shadow

Leaving

She closes the back door to the walled garden of childhood,
looks one last time at the sycamore she so often climbed,
its branches offering sanctuary.

Retraces her steps along the corridor of brown anaglypta
wallpaper, mounts the stairs, looks out to Parliament Hill Fields
and all those familiar churches where she had searched for Jesus.

Soon the house will spring into action, aunties fussing in the kitchen,
bridesmaids giggling in the bedrooms, her mother fixing her makeup.

She'll glide up the aisle of Holy Joe's in her finery make promises
pose for photographs cut wedding cake and the whole neighbourhood
will turn out to wave goodbye the bagwash lady the fishmonger,
the grocer, Mr Tether from the Haberdashery, the wife of the man
they are certain is a spy.

People will nod wisely and say what a handsome couple,
but when the last of the confetti finally falls from the windscreen
they'll be driving down Dartmouth Park Hill and she'll be leaning
on her husband's shoulder weeping.

Oh What a Lovely War – 1969

Her needle flies over tiny white gloves.
Stitches develop a regular rhythm,
she can almost hear the sound of marching feet.
Braid on bright blue hat and jacket, red pants,
a shiny metal helmet, a gleaming breast plate.
Fine nylon strings bring them all to life.

Now they bump along the road
in a Bedford Dormobile,
immaculate, neatly packed.
No muddy trenches for them,
off to the West Pier in Brighton
to take their place in the sun.

Extras play with parasols or eat ice cream.
The film crew balance on flimsy ladders,
"Camera. Action. Take one."
Jean Paul Cassell bangs the drum,
"Roll up, roll up, for the greatest show on earth."
Curtains open. Puppets take the stage.

The soldiers' rubber boots bob in time,
the captain jerks his bugle from his lips,
the French general sheathes his sword.
Only the old brown horse borrowed
from another show looks weary, while in the wings
a small platoon makes ready for their fate.

'A copper collection will take place
at the end of the performance'
says the writing on the wall.

Postman's Park

Lunch break

A brief hug
they seek a bench
unwrap sandwiches
cheese and pickle for him
crayfish and lettuce for her.

A solitary frayed
brown and white pigeon
struts about hoping
for abandoned crumbs.

A canopy of leaves
teased by the wind
like Japanese fan dancers.

A formal lawn

Sebastian methodically measures
bright orange netting like an artist
marking out his canvas.

Full of tools
one wheelbarrow stands
forks, spades, brushes, stakes.

His mate kneels at one corner
carefully sifting soil, troweling edges
his head bent, intent on perfection.

A third man brings in a barrow
rich green turf, all three
in harmony, finely tuned.

Postman's Park

most desirable des res
in the City half way up a tree
with a terracotta doorway

visitors rest in the shade
of the horse chestnut
soft tassels sway
to a secret tune

bunting heralds
a celebration

tours and the tiles
busy twitters

Madame Dulan
from Paris
scans the stories

a fan of wings
pigeons compete
for crumbs

dried grass flying past
a blue tit builds her nest

armoured woodlice
scramble
in dried bark

moths nest in flaky
circles of the tree trunk

Masako from Japan is moved
to write a haiku roughly translated
it says I recall a lot of persons
the flowers of today blossom

The Pew

I hope this is the pew where once the poet sat
having enjoyed his breakfast of burnt toast
sitting in his morning chair looking out to the graveyard
where his great grandfather is buried
drafting a letter then leaving his acorn
papered eyrie to saunter out of Cloth Fair
in his heavy coat and wide brimmed hat.

I hope this is the pew where once the poet sat
listening to sacred music from the deep throated organ
wafting through ancient pillars up to the ornate ceiling
looking up at the famous altar painting stored in Wales
during the war and now with the daylight flickering
on the angel with the chalice in Gethsemane
offering strength and courage to The Son of God.

I hope this is the pew where once the poet sat
next to the Wesley window that was not his favourite
near a memorial to someone's much loved daughter
and not far from the detailed deliberations
of Dame Anne Packington (widow) who in her will
in 1595 tried to devise ways to ensure her estate
would help the poor in perpetuity.

I hope this is the pew where once the poet sat
singing the hymns and half listening to the sermon
as thoughts of the letters he still had to write
and the women that he loved passed through his mind
having time to later wander to his favourite memorial
where it implies that it is not a man's ornate plaque
but the good deeds he accomplished that count.

In memory of Sir John Betjeman

Yellow balloon
(In memory of Dave)

Suppose I whispered the words *Postman's Park*
and wrote the word *love*
on a luggage label
and tied it to a yellow balloon.

as we watched it glide
a tad nearer to heaven
would you remember those happy days
at King Edward Building
sorting the mail and resting
between deliveries and where
colleagues became lifelong friends?

Haiku

growing/flowering
seeds/trees wither/dying
recycled benches

the banana fronds
flighty attention seekers
bring false promises

ciggy and the Sun
Joe's yellow anorak glows
then it's back to Barts.

The Handkerchief Tree

Scanning the Watts tiles
under the Loggia
what courage it must take
to jump in the depths
of Highgate Ponds
to save someone from drowning
to risk being crushed to death
by the weight of a runaway
horse's hooves
to die on a burning stairway
trying to save your mother
from a house on fire.

Is it all their gentle spirits turning
the leaves on the handkerchief tree
pure white in remembrance?

The Worm

On the path
I just avoid
stepping on a
brown worm.
I place him
on rain-sodden earth.
After all, anyone
can take
the wrong
direction.

King Alfred Building 1990

Sorting, walking
EC1 to EC4
big ones, small ones
white one, brown ones
Broadgate, Barbican
local stores.

Peabody flats in EC1
walking endless
flights of stairs
Hatton Garden
golden windows
jumping buses
countless fares.

Rest in park
before more sorting
deliveries that
must not fail
everything depends
on postmen
London's lifeblood
Royal Mail.

Metamorphosis

If I fell to the floor
my head bent
in supplication
would the moon
and Virgo be
making mischief?

If my hands
became thin and papery
like honesty pods
my muscles softened
would I have shrunk
to the size of pea?

If I felt a sensation
like pins and needles
giving me tiny legs,
but something dark
like a blackbird's wing
hovered over me,

would I know
instinctively, to
crawl into a crevice
as a droplet of my
human blood
painted my wings?

The Yellow House

A forest near Toulouse

The mist of mountains brings in tears of rain
Where charcoal burners sought to set up home
The forest floor is thick with fern again
Their labours lost, their bodies buried bone.
Strong men cut trees to feed the furnace mound
The smaller boughs formed shelters where they slept.
As darkness fell their families gathered round
So far from homes in Florence, woman wept.
Young men reap death on fields they did not sow
In Ypres, Verdun the slaughtered sons of France
The migrants had no choice of where to go,
But played their part where love then stood no chance.
In silent tribute to the dead we stand
Where ghosts are working still this unclaimed land.

A Model for Millais

Silver folds fall over her naked body.
He fastens clasps, traces her breasts
through the fine embroidered fabric
and leads her by the hand.

Nettles, pansies, petals.
Cadmium red, communion white.
Water seeps into her gown
her body motionless.

In fitful sleep her mind wanders.
Steely eyed snakes spit venom,
claws pounce on docile prey,
blood seeps into the forest floor.

Hours pass, light fades,
footsteps slither across the room.
Strong arms drag her swiftly
from the water.

The sun changes from orange
to dark red and then to purple.
Flowers still float on the surface.

Hockney

ride the pear blossom highway
photo-collage the Grand Canyon
feast on the season in Wetherby
mindful of memory
mark out clumps of trees
in charcoal on virgin paper
draw dark totems of death
soften your loss in Bridlington
delight in pale yellow flowers
through feathery foliage
make purple truly holy
take the bright pink path
to hypnotic woodland scenes
for music and ballet
on multiple screens

The Yellow House

She turned the corner and there she saw
the green shuttered house, the buttery yellow walls
radiating in the sun, the wind teasing the curtains,
the bright blue door.

How she had loved sipping tea in her friend's apartment,
sharing the drawings her brother had sent,
listening as she read his letters aloud
adding words of concern about his health.

She ordered a grenadine and soda in a nearby cafe
while a young woman, in fashionable dress
the curvaceous figure so favoured by artists
slumped into a chair nearby.

How she wished she was that kind of girl
loud, vivacious, set on filling her belly,
ready to be painted, pawed, seduced,
to pose in the afterglow of passion.

Then she caught sight of him, no mistaking
his heavy gait, body bent under the weight of his easel.
Slowly his feet walked passed her seat in the café.
Oh that flaming red hair. Heat filled her cheeks.

The Mistress - Brighton Museum

I float along a corridor of darkness and stop
where the moonlight shines on memory,

where my kitten heeled slippers still lie
topped with their circles of down.

In the eerie glow I can see the soft pink
satin circle where our rituals began.

You slowly rolling my silk stockings
down the length of my long legs,

the big blue velvet ribbon still tied into a bow
obscuring the trifle of a gown.

The white feather boa lifeless now
when once it floated above my head,

while naked I danced to the music
on the gramophone,

the patterns of the glass
from the chandelier creating

mischief

La Plage

When they bring the seaside to the banks of the Seine
mademoiselles in flimsy tops and tiny pants
flirt with les garçons, tongues lick Italian ice-cream
cool passion.
A clown twists balloons into floppy giraffes for children,
competing with the joys of running fully clothed through
huge spray mist showers.
People in panama hats and linen suits, eat oysters,
sip Sancerre, watch the bateaux bus swish past with the sun
screened tourists sagging in the heat.
Soon they'll bake on the steps of the Eiffel Tower, or queue
for the loo outside Notre Dame where the hot and bossy
attendant screams at those who don't have the exact change.
Some will head off to the Moulin Rouge to see the saucy
show girls, pearls of sweat falling from their breasts.
Office workers wet with perspiration will dive into the Metro
where an accordionist plays out his life to the tune of
'La Vie En Rose'
On the beach idle Parisiennes slide for one last time into the pool
when they bring the seaside to the banks of the Seine.

Paper Chain

Snow falls like flakes of memory
tucked under a warm blanket

cheeks pinched with cold
the window a filigree frost

rough sawn logs stacked in the grate
a comforting casserole in the oven

the smell of honeyed baked apples
stuffed with raisins

'Gales in the Hebrides, snow expected
to continue in the Highlands'

Mr Crick the newsagent hanging a single
dusty paper-chain in his window

Busy sparrows in a flurry of snow
spinning on the bird feeder

Mrs Kettle in her cottage with her goat
and cat huddle together to keep warm

The letter 'We are sorry your great
 aunt died two months ago.

We are sure she would
have liked your letter returned herein.'

Ghosts

The house is rocking in the wind
torrential rain blotting out the landscape
a cold breeze creeping under the patio door
ghosts calling from the loft.
Left the curtains closed on purpose.
Now the room feels warmer
things I had forgotten shout for attention
the threadbare Eeyore on the chest of drawers
the wooden horse on wheels that never
got to the charity shop.
Alan's father in full uniform
in a brass frame and the books
rows and rows of them.

The Rue des Abbesses

rain laden leaves of the plane trees hover
over the cobbled square of Place des Abbesses
half way up the hill to Montmartre,
where the art nouveau Metro stands
nearby artists in the past enjoyed a glass of absinthe
the licorice tang on the tongue mingling with the woody
taste of Gauloise watching the thin plumes
of smoke rise before their journey up the hill
buskers' accordions would bleat sad songs
where once blousy tarts with bright red lips
and bulging breasts lolled in doorways waiting
for lizard-like pimps full of empty promises
further up the cobbled street withered nuns
in warm robes hurry to light candles
pray for the day of redemption
in the solid white stone of the Sacré Coeur
while nearby tourists gather
with phones and camcorders
seeking out gaudy copies of Van Gogh
or to stand for a silhouette fashioned for 25 euros
before sliding down the hill on the funicular
to the Moulin Rouge, where a glass of champagne
is a rip off and showgirls ply their trade
sweating like leaves laden with rain.

Wading Through Treacle

The doors are locked and
it's that journey with someone chasing you and
you climb out of the window and
you sneak a quick look back but can't really see and
you're on the roof of a shaking train and
sweating with fear and
you try and wake up and
you do and
that's in the dream too and
then it happens again and
in the morning you read one of those dream books and
it tells you what you already know and
how we are all trapped in some sort of unreality and
even if we are in happy relationships and
our kids are not on drugs or benefits and
it's then that you notice the home made jams in the cupboard and
realise they are two years old and
you've been meaning to clear them out for months and
that's because of the Oscars and
the bad weather that's coming and
for most of our lives we are wading through treacle.

The Ash Tree

from an ancient wood trapped in the garden of a terrace
in South London was the reason I bought the house. I
imagined it whispering words of comfort and even singing
to me if things got tough. As the seasons passed I watched
from my bedroom window, sparrows, blackbirds and
occasionally a bright red woodpecker. The new
green growth appeared in spring, giving way to leafy
summer shade, the shedding of autumn leaves, the snow
covered its bare branches in winter.

The dry earth around its roots became a secret den for the
children, its weathered trunk created footholds inviting feet
to climb, sturdy ropes supported a swing and a wooden tree
house perched amongst its foliage. Only once did I cautiously
climb it's twisted trunk to rescue a terrified cockatiel in a
torrential storm.

Boys

you bounce through the door, spiky hair,
easy smile, I try to buy you a meal, you protest
we settle for lattes and pieces of quiche

we flick through the exhibition brochure
featuring the head of a man in eternal damnation
you talk of your son who hasn't rung all week

whisper how much you miss him, calling
him in the morning, the night time hug
but we both know it's so much more than this

re-visiting Pythagoras for him, revving your motor
bikes down the bumpy lane, showing him
how to set a barrel in case he ever works in a bar

soon we'll marvel at ancient treasures, watch
films about furnaces, gaze at fishermen
sifting through nets for a Satyr's metal leg

we'll mooch round Fortnums, buy posh sea salt
in the basement, wander through Green Park
hug in the sun, say goodbye at Victoria.

Sprinkling ashes

The sound of a lament from an upstairs window
I make my way to the museum of Toulouse-Lautrec,
my father's favourite painter, canvases of dancers,
orange faces, frilly suspenders and the town
where I sprinkled his ashes in the Tarn twenty years ago.

I eat mussels in the square with chilled white wine,
will myself down to the river again, watch a fisherman
cast his line, sleep a while in the sunshine, build a boat
to send my mother's ashes downstream to join my father's.

As night falls the man in the moon hides his features,
the stars sparkle like sequins on my mother's favourite
evening gown. The river pounds like horse's hooves
on hard ground and lanterns light the way back home.

A Valiant Brood

Prolonged wintry weather savaged the bees
despite honey stocks and bee fondant
wind rain and snow penetrated
their sturdy wooden hive.
Now they lie in tiny icy cocoons
clustered around their queen
a valiant brood
that did all it could
to stay alive.

The Tortoise

when the tortoise crawls out of hibernation
from the box of straw, do the rings of his ancient shell
shield him from regret
does his wrinkly head recall the sound of her voice
the haunting echo of her wild, warm laugh
as he takes his first bite into a lettuce leaf
are tortoises bereft of feeling
is that the secret of their long life?

Timeless

As snow transforms foliage into icy fingers
the bus crawls caterpillar-like up the hill
the seagulls' feet thump on our flat bedroom roof
and greenfinches wait in an orderly queue
to swing on bird feeders in our cherry tree
and hymns of the faithful reach a crescendo.

You are propped up on clouds of white fluffy pillows
knowing that your life is coming to an end
later we watch shafts of silver light
pirouette over the dark green ribbons of the sea
like a final performance, dancing dancing
to that final bow and rapturous applause.

Acknowledgments

With love to my long suffering partner, Alan, for fixing food, the photocopier and the computer, not necessarily in that order. With love to Robin and Sheila, Paul and Caroline, and grandchildren Joshua, Jamie and Nicky.

Heartfelt thanks to John McCullough for mentoring, Jackie Wills, tutors and fellow students at The Poetry School, Arvon, New Writing South and Anne-Marie at Troubadour for their inspiration and encouragement. Thanks also to Simon, Robin, Maggie and poets from my 'Pop In and Write Poetry' workshops for their support.

Heartfelt thanks to Kiersty Boon for her technical skills and endless patience.

Ann Perrin

Ann Perrin was born in the blitz. Her parents became marionette makers and performers after the war as 'Ron and Joan Field's Marionettes.' Ann lived in a creative household, which meant that her formal education was often disrupted.

As a teenager, Ann followed in their footsteps working in Variety on the same bill as Max Miller and Morecambe and Wise. She worked for TV on 'The Telegoons.' Ann and her family made and performed with their marionettes in the film 'Oh What a Lovely War,' filmed on Brighton's West Pier.

Later, as a single parent, she decided to train as a teacher. She taught gypsies and art in a comprehensive school, studied for a BA with the Open University. She was a senior manager in adult education in Lambeth, wrote a play 'Travelling Nowhere,' which was performed at the Young Vic and studied part-time for an M.Sc. Ann retrained as a therapist working for Primary Care Trusts and also became carer to her mother. She is a member of the Society of Women Writers and Journalists.

Ann started writing poetry later in life and has had poems published in Compact, Writing News and anthologies, and won a competition judged by New Writing South in 2014. She was a poet in residence in Postman's Park in the City of London in 2015, thanks to the Poetry School and London Parks and Gardens Trust. She has read her poems in London at Troubadour, Lumen, the House of Vans and other venues in Brighton, including Pighog.